PERFECT PARTIES

A Guide to
Successful Entertaining

Mary Gostelow

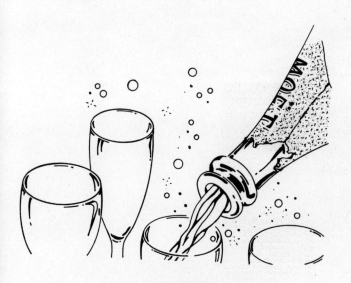

B T BATSFORD LTD
LONDON

ISBN 0 7134 4881 4

Typeset by Progress Filmsetting
and printed in Great Britain by
Butler & Tanner Ltd
Frome, Somerset
for the publishers
B T Batsford Ltd
4 Fitzhardinge Street
London W1H 0AH

CONTENTS

INTRODUCTION

Everyone loves a good party, be it an organized affair or a spontaneous happening. I am lucky—I travel a tremendous amount and I see different kinds of parties all over the world.

Here are my own notes on parties. I describe some of my favourite occasions, and there are lots of tips for children's parties, picnics and entertaining the boss. Have fun!

I should like to offer special thanks to my partner Wendy Lees and my husband Martin Gostelow. The many others who have shared expertise and to whom I give my thanks include:

The Champagne Bureau, Malcolm McIntyre and Alison Pendree; Caroline Conran; Fleur Cowles; Dr Joan Freeman; Allison Guertin; Mireille Guiliano; Jennifer (Mrs Betty Kenward); Patricia Hodge; Kingsway Public Relations and Jane Howard; Roland Klein; Diana May; Moët & Chandon, Henri Perrier Moët and Nancy Jarratt; Claudia Roden; Carole Rothstein; Peter Townend; Jan Vachule; and Hilary Wharton. The drawings are by Linda Sandey.

Chapter One

WHAT MAKES A GOOD PARTY?

It could be said that when two or more people gather together a party is possible. I personally remember many marvellous occasions getting to know a special man. We used to go sunset-watching from the hills around Marlborough. Potted shrimps, home-made brown bread, a bottle of wine and two glasses...and we had a party.

A party requires:

People, of whom one is generally in charge (i.e. the host) and the others guests
Some kind of food and drink
A setting (ambience)

Those are the ingredients. Combined with panache, they can produce a good party.

Money has intentionally been left out of the main essentials. Some of the best parties may be those where lemon drink is served from plastic cups in a house bereft of all furniture except packing cases. If the flair is there, the party can still work magnificently.

Some people put a lot of thought, effort and money into a party and it still does not succeed. I have been to plenty of big functions with elaborate flower arrangements and other expensive accessories. People have spent a fortune on clothes and hairstyles and somehow it has all been rather boring.

Sometimes too much obvious organization can work against a party. One of the secrets is covert attention to planning so that, when the party happens, it seems to do so all by itself.

Why not spare a few moments to write down the names of those people who you think give good parties?

....

....

....

Now, think about *why* their parties work. What is their secret? They probably have many of the qualities outlined in Chapter Two.

You may, of course, be all by yourself. That should not stop you having a party. *Enjoy yourself.* Why should you deprive yourself of a pleasurable occasion? As columnist Lynda Lee-Potter once said, 'Perfection...is a glass of champagne and the latest Jeffrey Archer.'

Generally, though, guests are essential to making a party work. Write down here the six people you would most like to invite to a party:

....

....

....

....

....

....

Think about why they are good guests—and look at Chapter Three.

Ambience

A high-cost party in a bleak hall starts off bleakly. By contrast, a casual supper in a warm candlelit room has a welcoming feel to it.

Where the party is held is a necessary ingredient, and the organizer should think about:

1 Suitability of size, location, amenities (seating) and car-parking. Sometimes you cannot do anything about suitability. We live in a tiny cottage and it is impractical to have a large dinner party. When we

first moved there I used to invite as many as twelve, but it was terribly hugger-mugger and there was not enough room for chairs. Now we face reality and stick to a maximum of eight (which has the added advantage of ensuring better conversations with each guest).

2 Possible decoration of the chosen place. Unlike a personal relationship, which matures, ambience needs to make an *immediate impact.* Have nightlights as guests arrive, and later turn on ordinary lights. Who cares if your Christmas decorations fall down half-way through the evening? As long as they looked good at the beginning, that is all that matters.

Remember, a party needs to start well. And ambience is the first element of the occasion that greets the guests.

Chapter Two
THE HOST

————— ❧❦❧ —————

Fleur Cowles is one of the most experienced and popular international hosts. She was official American representative at the Coronation: many of her friends around the world are household names.

Fleur Cowles says:

> The *first* thing I do when planning a dinner is to add the element of surprise—trying not to gather the same familiar faces (no matter how attractive). Guests now expect to meet someone new—and *do*. London is the crossroads of the world today, so such surprises can come from far-flung places—friends I made in art, literature and the political world and from incessant travel; they help me cast an evening with unexpected people.

> *Two:* I have a good mix—wherever possible inviting *opposites:* the more divergent their views, the more successful the talk. Conversation never flags. To this end, I only have round dining tables in any of my homes. This way, a meal tends to end up with *general* table talk. Even the shyest shine with unexpected views.

> Luckily, in England clashes in viewpoints seldom if ever end in clashes of friendship. The best examples come from Parliament: even Winston Churchill used to walk out of the House of Commons with his arm around the bitter opponent of a preceding bellicose debate (often Aneurin Bevan).

> *Three:* I insist on non-pretentious food, if for no better reason than to guarantee it will be piping hot; decoration must not be allowed to win over taste. Such unnecessary elaborations as one vegetable served inside another, or pheasant tails decorating the birds take precious time and

are best left to Embassy kitchens. *Cool* food is no compliment.

Four: if I do not feel at ease, I find my concern is passed on to the guests. I avoid this by carefully thinking out every detail of the evening and by seeing that staff are well informed beforehand. Then I become one of my own guests.

Five: I never invite a person I do not genuinely like—and guests know this. Besides, I know no-one skilful enough to hide a secret dislike from others. One tiny drop can poison an evening. Another thing: paying off obligations by inviting unlikeable people to dine is a dangerous business. Send flowers instead.

My golden rule: whatever the circumstances or the guest list, act normal, be normal, be relaxed, be glad your friends are with you. Enjoy their company.

Here is a sample dinner menu:

Beignets of halibut (sauce faintly curried)
Roast poussins (a tiny half to each guest, served on fried bread with finely minced fried mushrooms) and seasonal fresh vegetables
Whole poached peaches (serve diced ginger and ginger sauce with them, cream on the side)

(One of Fleur Cowles's many beautiful books is: *Flower Game*, Collins.)

Well, we cannot all emulate Fleur Cowles, but organization helps any party-giver.

Party Book

The organized host carefully records who came to which party, on what occasion, what food was served (plus other relevant details such as 'Jack sat next to Jill and he spent the entire evening trying to get her to go up the hill that weekend'—i.e. do not put Jack next to Jill again!).

The party book is a modern version of the traditional butler's *pantry book* concept. Here were written down all details about guests' eating habits and other likes and dislikes, so that when, perhaps many years later, the guests were asked again, they would find all their

penchants accurately remembered. (Today, butlers/
administrators might computerize all such valuable
information.)

You might like to start your own party book. Buy a
plain notebook and use the headings format below (or,
if you are compterized, input in similar style).

Your party book needs to record:

Date
Celebration
Place
People (with addresses/telephone numbers if you do
not already know them)
Food
Drinks
Seating plan (where relevant)
Things to remember

Solo Entertaining

There is nothing to stop the single person giving parties
just as if there were two or more hosts. Sometimes my
husband has to go away unexpectedly on business and I
am left to cope. If this happens I never cancel any
invitations.

I used not to tell guests that I would be alone in case
they felt it would be too much trouble for me as lone
host. Now I feel they would rather know beforehand.

As lone host, I find it especially important to plan a
menu that requires the minimum last-minute preparation. It is easiest, at a supper party, to plan a simple
roast; there will always be someone to help carve if you
are not confident of your own prowess.

A single host of either sex can count on much more
help from guests. Do not be offended if guests offer to
bring part of the meal. Take them up on it!

As far as drinks are concerned, simplicity is again
important. If you are offering an open bar before a
meal, put all the drinks out so that people can help

themselves—or, alternatively, appoint someone 'barman'.

Staff

If you think you cannot cope, admit that you need someone to help. In the case of some of the special parties mentioned later (children's parties, for instance), it is more or less essential to have several helpers.

If you are having friends to supper and you want kitchen help, here are some ideas:

1 Ask a friend's daughter or son if they would like pocket money (check with their parents first that this will not affect their school work).
2 If you have a cleaning help, see if she would like to come in for a couple of hours (pay much more than you would for daytime work and make sure that she has transport both ways).
3 Hire outside help. For a big party, you could employ trained staff.

If you are employing a butler, you might find you get a woman! The butlers' supremo, Ivor Spencer, suggests that suitable dress for a woman butler is a below-knee skirt and blouse for day, and a long unobtrusive gown (no cleavage) for night.

How to Get Rid of Guests

It does sometimes happen, even to the best hosts. Some people just do not know when to go.

The host has to be gracious when speeding departures. I remember an informal surprise birthday party in Beirut some years ago. The birthday man was obviously not amused and made it quite clear to everyone after about half an hour that he wanted them to go. This was embarrassing for all the guests—and for his wife, who had gone to a lot of trouble to surprise him.

If you are host and someone does not seem inclined to leave, here are some ideas:

1 Tactfully ask if he/she has transport home and, if not, offer to call a taxi.

2 Say quite truthfully that *(a)* you have to be up early tomorrow morning; *(b)* you have a dentist's appointment; *(c)* someone is waiting for you. Do not lie. If your guest cannot sense when an occasion should come to an end, you are quite at liberty to be honest.
3 Ask for help with the washing-up, and then do not sit down again afterwards.

If none of these ploys works and Stanley Stayer is still around, try some of the techniques that Clement Freud discovered in restaurants when he did a series on 'How to get thrown out of restaurants'.

You could:

1 Start sweeping the floor/using a noisy vacuum cleaner.
2 If the guest, by now definitely unwanted, is sitting at a table, remove the table.
3 Turn out the lights.

As a last resort, call the police!

Note: if you are a lone woman and you suspect that Stanley Stayer might stay on, unwanted, afterwards, pre-empt the situation. Before everyone else leaves, ask Stanley if he has transport home and do everything you can to make sure that he leaves with the others. If he does not get the hint, ask someone else to stay on a little longer.

Chapter Three
THE GUEST

----------◦◦◦◦----------

(*Warning:* this next section is a sermon. But do take
time to read it through. Some of the most surprising
people—successful in all other aspects of life—are not
good guests because they have not bothered to learn.)

The good guest is full of '*re*'s. The good guest should be
reliable (and yet unpredictable), *relaxed, responsible*
and *responsive.*

Reliability

If asked to a party, the good guest always turns up at an
approximately appropriate time.

As guest, you will be most appreciated if your host
knows he can rely on your contribution to the party.

At the same time, a certain degree of unpredictability,
in the form of spontaneity, is desirable. Nothing is
worse than the guest who always turns up in the same
navy-blue dress, or the guest who always say at 10.30
'Well, I think we should be going, Cedric' (you long for
her to wait until 10.35 to make her predictable
announcement).

Relaxation

Try not to be edgy and nervous. If you are hungry and
there is no sign of food coming do not twist your hands.
If necessary, concentrate on tensing and relaxing
muscles which do not show, to relieve stress (perhaps
push the balls of your feet down into the ground).

Enjoy yourself. This is one reason you were asked to

the party! You are in someone else's hands until you leave.

Responsibility

This category is your commitment to your host. By accepting his invitation you have morally bound yourself to behave to a certain level.

This may involve not getting drunk. It may consist of the onerous task of making conversation all evening with someone's mother who speaks not a word of your own language and suffers from halitosis into the bargain.

You accepted the invitation. You have to do your duty for the duration of the event.

If this involves having to show initiative, again do your duty. If someone has unexpectedly to take charge, it is the good guest who comes to the rescue.

Responsiveness

Guests should follow the lead of their host. If the party turns into a theatrical evening, guests should enter into the mood and throw themselves into whatever is happening. If a host suggests going swimming, and no-one has any proper gear, it is the guests who nonetheless plunge in who come up trumps in everyone's eyes, and it is they who will be asked again.

Local Custom

If you are asked to a party in unfamiliar territory, do your homework:

1 If you are asked for a certain time, what time should you turn up?
2 Do you take a gift?
3 What is customary departure time?
4 What kind of thank-you afterwards is common?

Throughout the *Middle East,* for instance, if you are asked for a certain time no-one will expect you to turn up until at least an hour after that—perhaps more. You should take a gift, and be prepared for it not to be opened in front of you. In some parts of *Florida* you should turn up exactly on the minute for which you were asked. If it is a dinner party, you can expect several cocktails (no-one will mind if you ask for wine) and lots of hearty snacks, including whole cheeses. Finally dinner will be served. You can leave more or less the moment the meal is finished.

Throughout *France* you will find pre-dinner drinking is less lengthy. Cheese is part of the main meal, served before dessert. In *England,* on the other hand, cheese is customarily served after dessert. In the *Netherlands,* local gin, drunk neat, and sherry are the most popular pre-dinner drinks. In *Australia* you might expect beer—and get excellent wines.

Gifts

To give or not to give is a local custom. In some areas guests automatically take a small gift to any party. In others it is not the done thing. If you are not sure, play safe and take a small flower bouquet. You do not want to start a trend: it is very easy to get into the habit with certain people of having to take gifts because they always bring something to you.

In this day and age, do not give chocolates unless you are *sure* the host will appreciate them.

Do not give over-elaborate presents. I remember my jeweller many years ago in the Middle East, who once arrived merely for coffee bearing a cake a good two feet across lavishly embellished with my name.

How to Leave

If you think it is time to go, you should generally go—although there are exceptions to this rule.

In some areas it is etiquette for the most senior person to prompt departure. Obviously if you are in the presence of an important person it is not up to you to lead the exit.

In general, however, there is no point in staying at a party long after you can afford the time (or perhaps want) to be there. Do not make a fuss about leaving. Simply try to get your host to one side and say how sorry you are to have to go and you want to slip out quietly. There is no reason why everyone else's enjoyment should be ruined by your precipitate departure.

Thank-Yous

As with gifts, these are a matter of local custom. From my own point of view the best thank-yous are personal notes written the following day and posted first class. Such notes specifically mention features of the event. Next in order of courtesy comes the telephone call on the following day. Bottom of my rating comes the first-class letter sent a month after the event, simply 'thanking me for the party', so that it is quite obvious that the writer waited until the end of the month and went through her diary writing all her thank-yous, without even remembering what was what.

Even after a formal invitation a personal letter is in order. Some people greatly value anything that is handwritten.

Thank-You Gifts

It may be that a small thank-you gift is in order. Perhaps you are unable to repay hospitality. In some countries, indeed, it is customary to send follow-up presents. Flowers are always appreciated if the host is at home, but are no good if the person who gave your party last night has now left for his business trip to Auckland.

Chapter Four
EXPENSE

How you spend on your party depends on you, your budget and the event.

Some people never budget for parties. 'A party is a party and I just buy whatever I need.' Others plan beforehand and carefully itemize.

Here is a pre-party budget plan.

1 Write down the function, where and when it will be held and the number of people present.
....
2 How much do you think you can afford?
3 Now itemize all anticipated expenses (some may not be relevant, in which case leave a blank)
   (a) Preparation (publicity, invitations)
   (b) Ambience
   (c) Transport
   (d) Clothes, beauty, make-up
   (e) Catering
   (f) Drink
   (g) Food (itemize all requirements
       separately and simply enter total)
   (h) Utilities
   (i) Entertainment
   (j) Other (babysitting, security)   _____

                    TOTAL   _____

4 You may be surprised how much higher **3** is than your original **2** figure. If this is the case, can you raise your budget, or should you lower your sights and have a less ambitious party?

21

5 Whatever happens, if you do have a budget try to stick within it. There are always some incidental extras so, if these happen before the event, try to economize elsewhere. There may be an accident at the event—say a broken glass—and you may prefer not to count this in your accounts.

6 After the event, why not go through and itemize what you really did spend?

(a) Preparation (publicity, invitations)

(b) Ambience

(c) Transport

(d) Clothes, beauty, make-up

(e) Catering

(f) Drink

(g) Food (itemize all requirements
      separately and simply enter total)

(h) Utilities

(i) Entertainment

(j) Other (babysitting, security)   _____

                              TOTAL   _____

Chapter Five

PREPARATION

------------------------•◦❈◦•------------------------

Sometimes the best parties are the informal last-minute occasions that work *because* they are spontaneous. There is, however, no half-way stage. You should either prepare as thoroughly as possible— or not at all.

Preparation includes the following:

1 Deciding that you want a party.
2 Setting day, time and place.
3 Establishing your guest list and sending out invitations.
4 Planning food and drink.
5 Thinking about your own dress and grooming.
6 Decorating the setting (where necessary).
7 Making sure that everything is ready on time.

Points 1-3 will probably be settled at the same time, some way ahead of the date. If you leave the arrangements too late you might find that you cannot get the venue you want—if you are planning a party away from home—and your desired guests are already booked elsewhere.

Lists can be invaluable. Write everything down at each stage of the party planning—this where your own party book can be a help (see page 12).

It really is most important to make sure that everything is ready on time. Allow for unexpected delays. Do not count on catching a train that should get you to your house five minutes before everyone arrives. As a typical quirk of fate, that will be the one night when there is an hour's delay.

As host, try to be ready ahead of time.

Host's Final Relaxation Recipe

Plan to be ready a full 15 minutes before everyone arrives. Some people now find it is a good idea to sit down with a pre-party drink (careful!) or read the daily paper (for another reason, take care—newsprint can blacken hands and clothes). A much safer and more relaxing way of spending the final quarter of an hour before a party is this:

1 Check everything is ready. Is the oven on (if necessary)? (Total: three minutes.)
2 Now why not do a short exercise routine? Stand up, legs apart. Stretch your arms out and up. Breathe deeply. Count slowly to ten. Bring your arms up, elbows bent, in front of you and twist as far as you can round to the left and then to the right. Do this five times. With elbows bent and arms still in front of you, count slowly to ten. Legs together. Shake each leg alternately five times. Stand still, looking at a particular item in the room—and count to ten slowly. (Total: three minutes.)
3 You should still have nine minutes in hand. Check your appearance in the mirror, put on perfume (if appropriate) and now get a drink and sit and wait for your guests.

Chapter Six

INVITATIONS

————◦◦◦◦————

Timing

I am coming to the conclusion that it never hurts to send invitations out in plenty of time. It is better to be too soon than too late.

Here are some suggested guidelines for timings:

Children's parties—two weeks ahead
Cocktail parties—three weeks ahead
Dinner parties—four weeks ahead
Important family gatherings—as far in advance as possible
Informal suppers—three weeks ahead
Weddings—at least six weeks ahead

Types of Invitation

There are one or two salient points to remember when inviting people:

1 Generally an informal invitation implies an informal party. Do not invite people verbally to a black-tie formal dinner.
2 Invitations should state:
host
date
place
time
dress (unless obvious)
cause of celebration (if relevant)
3 Unless you are sure of the efficiency and reliability of the guests concerned, bear in mind the fact that invitations may not be written down and remembered.

Invitations should be answered like to like. Here, therefore, are the alternatives:

Printed Invitations

You will find your printer can advise on suitable wording. A typical printed card might read:

Mrs John Smith

At Home

to meet her father-in-law, Mr Justus Smith

Saturday 3 December 1990

RSVP   Dinner 8.00 for 8.30 p.m.
49 Smith Square   Black Tie
London SW1

Notes

1 The host will *handwrite* the name of the guest at the top of the card.
2 The guest should reply, in handwriting (not typing), following a similar format. Do not under any circumstances buy a commercial acceptance or refusal card. Regardless of how well you know Jane Smith, if the invitation came from Mrs John Smith and she handwrote your name as 'Mr and Mrs Bernard Bloggs', you should reply as follows:

> Mr and Mrs Bernard Bloggs thank Mrs John Smith for her kind invitation to meet her father-in-law, Mr Justus Smith on Saturday 3 December 1990, and accept with great pleasure.

or:

> Mr and Mrs Bernard Bloggs thank Mrs John Smith for her kind invitation to meet her father-in-law, Mr Justus Smith on Saturday 3 December 1990, but much regret they are already engaged that evening.

Bought Invitations

A variety of different printed invitations can be purchased. There are spaces for you to write in specific details.

Note: If you are sent a bought invitation, you can buy an acceptance or refusal card, but you would do better to handwrite your reply in similar wording. If the invitation is formal, follow the guidelines given under 'Printed Invitations'. If the invitation is informal, follow the guidelines under 'Informal Invitations'.

Informal Invitations

These should be handwritten and generally follow these lines:

29 January 19—

Dear Jenny,
Are you free to come and have supper on Monday evening, 21 February? My father-in-law will be with us and I should so much like him to meet you both. Martin and Mary are coming. Informal, 7.30 p.m.—do hope you can make it.

Yours,

Antoinette

Notes

1 You should reply to such invitation by a handwritten letter, ideally sent first-class and as soon as possible.

2 February 19—

Dear Antoinette,
Thank you so much for your kind invitation for supper on Monday 21 February. We should love to come and meet your father-in-law. It will be fun, too, to see you both again, and to renew acquaintance with Martin and Mary. Many thanks for thinking of us.

With all good wishes

Yours,

Jenny

Children's Invitations

You can buy attractive invitation cards that the small guests will enjoy receiving—or you can make your own (see page 62).

INVITATIONS

Note: it is essential that all invitations to children's parties state the time of the party's *end,* as well as the beginning.

* * *

When you receive an invitation, make a note in your diary. Keep the invitation safely, and take it along with you to the party just in case you lose you way *en route* and have to telephone!

Chapter Seven
FOOD

(For foods for specific occasions such as weddings, see the appropriate sections of the book.)

I asked Jane Howard, Director of the Catering Market Division, Kingsway Public Relations, for advice on party food in general. 'Generally food exists to complement the party, not to dominate it, and certainly not to dominate *you*. A little practical planning will help avoid this,' she told me.

Here are Jane's tips for catering for your party:

1 Cook to suit *your personality*. It is an obvious point, but often overlooked. Prepare something you like and that you can cook well. Never try a dish for the first time as it involves too many uncertainties.
2 Cook to suit *your guests*. Select something most people will enjoy and which they will feel confident about eating. Avoid eels, offal, spicy curries and food requiring chopsticks unless you are sure people can cope.
3 Cook to suit *your facilities*. Remember the size of your kitchen and what equipment is available.
4 Cook to suit the *service situation*. If everyone is seated at a table, with cutlery and condiments, you can serve food that requires more careful handling. If you are planning a stand-up buffet, remember that everyone will have to balance a plate and drink, so make items easy to manage.
5 Cook to suit *your home*. This is a selfish but highly practical point and one always to consider. Pick recipes that will not spill all over your carpet. Avoid spaghetti in a buffet. Do not have any dishes or utensils so hot that they may mark table or other surfaces.

6 Cook to suit *your budget*. A sensible balance of dishes will keep the costs down. Many party favourites—like garlic bread and jacket-baked potatoes—are inexpensive and will help to bulk out the menu. Many 'peasant' dishes like chilli and pizza also fit into this category, but check beforehand that guests will like them (many older people, in particular, would prefer an alternative).

7 Cook to suit *yourself*. If you want to spend the party in the kitchen, pick a delicate, difficult and probably impressive dish. If you prefer to be eating and talking with your guests, find something which requires less attention. The 'peasant' dishes mentioned earlier are perfect—as, indeed, is most traditional, provincial cooking.

Professional Catering

You may, of course, decide to hand over the whole thing to professionals. The advantages include the fact that you can then relax and enjoy your party, and that you know beforehand how much it is going to cost (make sure you get a definite quotation covering all items). However, you cannot claim that it was all 'home cooking' and, anyway, if you are careful, you should be able to undercut the professionals who, after all, have to claim their time and still make money.

I asked Jane Howard to share some professional tips that might save the home caterer money.

'If you are thinking about any large-scale event,' she said, 'approach the problems as a professional caterer would.'

1 *Food supply.* Retail packs of anything are expensive compared to cash-and-carry or wholesaler sizes. Freezer centres fall in between. Some cash-and-carry centres demand proof that you are a bona fide trader, in which case you may find you know someone who can buy for you. Most trade wholesalers will supply food in minimum drops which are fine for a medium-sized party upwards. Read catering magazines for sources of supply.

2 *Convenience v. freshly prepared foods.* Labour-saving dishes abound, and it is often wise selectively to incorporate a few, both to widen the available menu choice and to reduce your workload. Frozen is not the opposite of fresh, and many catering companies supply high-quality starters, entrées and desserts (most will be available through wholesalers). Items like prepared pâtés, battered onion rings, breaded mushrooms, gâteaux, cheesecakes and pies can all help stretch your menu at moderate cost and to great effect.

3 *Disposables.* There are many excellent, sturdy and attractive disposable plates, knives, forks and napkins available. As long as they are strong enough, no-one will mind their use and you will be relieved of the dreary post-party clear-up.

4 *Delegate.* If guests are willing to help, let them. Do, however, allocate defined tasks. This keeps the work progressing smoothly and efficiently and allows people to sit down with a clear conscience when they have finished their job.

5 *It is your party.* Keep the catering in order and in perspective, and you, and everyone else, will have much more fun.

Chapter Eight
DRINK
(See also 'Cocktail Parties')

Do make sure that you have enough drink. It is better to have too much than too little but, by the same token, do not show how much you have (or it might all be drunk!). It is a good thing always to have some drink in reserve.

If you want advice on what to serve and how much you need, go along to your local off-licence or liquor store. You will find that people there probably have more time to talk than their counterparts in a large supermarket (and you may be able to borrow glasses free of charge).

Note: always have plenty of non-alcoholic drinks. Increasingly today—for reasons of driving laws and health—some people prefer soft drinks.

Serving
Do make sure drinks are at the right temperature:

Spirits can be room temperature. Mixers can either be chilled in the refrigerator or you may prefer to offer ice separately. Do not assume that all your guests want ice: to serve ice in a Scotch whisky is anathema to many connoisseurs.

Red wines (apart from new Beaujolais, served chilled) are usually served at room temperature. Open the bottle at least half an hour before serving. Only decant if there is sediment in the bottle.

White wines are normally served slightly chilled, from the fridge.

When pouring, hold a wine bottle by the neck.

Glasses

I hate metal 'glasses', and anything too highly decorated. Ideally, I like the thinnest possible glass. Red wine glasses normally have a bulbous bowl to allow air to reach the surface. White wine glasses are often tall and slim, with slim stems to allow you to hold the glass without touching—and warming—the wine in the bowl.

Champagne

Bottle sizes

Quarter-bottle (split)	187 ml
Half-bottle	375 ml
Standard bottle	750 ml
Magnum (2 bottles)	1.5 l
Jeroboam (4 bottles)	3 l
Methusalem (8 bottles)	6 l
Salmanazar (12 bottles)	9 l

Serving

Champagne should never be served ice-cold as over-chilling masks the delicate bouquet. Ideal bottle temperature is 42-48°F. Achieve this by standing the bottle for 30 minutes in an ice bucket (or plastic bucket) half-filled with a mixture of ice and water.

Use slender glass flutes or tulip-shaped glasses (some *cognoscenti* use a narrow rounded flute, with a slight waist towards the top to retain the bouquet). Do not use flat *coupes,* which should be reserved for ice-cream sundaes.

A champagne bottle contains up to 90 lb of pressure per square inch! Open it carefully. Unwind and remove the wire muzzle. Grasp the cork in one hand and the bottle in the other at an angle of 45 degrees *away from you and everyone else.* Slowly twist the bottle — not the cork. When the cork is out, keep the bottle at a 45-degree angle for a few seconds to allow surplus gas to escape.

Ideally, you should pour champagne holding the bottle by the bottom identation (the punt). Pour about an inch into each glass and then half-fill.

Many other sparkling wines are also excellent. I am particularly fond of some Spanish cavas, and such Californian 'champagnes' as those produced by Château St Jean, Domaine Chandon, Hanns Kornell, and Schramsberg.

Chapter Nine

ENTERTAINMENT

Music

Music is the obvious entertainment at any kind of party, be it the Bournemouth Sinfonietta playing in your garden or a tape of musical bumps for your youngest's third birthday party.

Live music is a delight—if it is *good*. Please do not inflict Uncle Alfred's piano playing on everyone just because you are so proud that he never even played a note until last month.

If you want good live music for your party and you do not know where to find it, ask your local orchestra or music society if they have one or two members who would like to play for you. Be prepared to pay a lot for professional musicians, and make sure that they enjoy the occasion. Treat them as guests. If they are playing in concert, make sure that everyone is comfortably seated and that there are no interruptions during the music. If they are providing background music, make sure everyone can hear them but, conversely, that they are not too loud.

As far as taped music is concerned, it is generally a good idea to keep it fairly quiet. Think of your guests when making your choice. Do not greet your guests with *Rigoletto* just because you are a Verdi fan.

Depending on the atmosphere you want to create for an adults' party, you could play 1930s dance bands, traditional jazz, or Mozart divertimenti, which were actually written as background music.

Note: if you have a noisy disco, make sure there is a 'quiet room' as well.

Party Games

Even adults love party games at times, but this places a great responsibility on the host, who must either organize a full-scale 'games party' and let everyone know about it beforehand, and dress appropriately, or decide spontaneously on games just as coffee is finishing.

If you do decide on a full-scale games party, only invite people who enjoy the *thought* of playing games. Most people enjoy it when it actually happens, but some squirm with trepidation beforehand.

As host, give your guests an indication of what they should wear (wellington boots, low-cleavage or what?). It might be a good idea to ask them each to bring along an idea for a game, and any props that are necessary.

You may have to be unusually bossy to get the games started. When the games begin to 'take off', you can relax.

Here is one of my favourite games. Everyone is paired, and one person from each couple is given a lavatory roll. He or she has to wrap the other, standing up, in mummy form, without breaking the roll. When the mummies are completed, the host announces solemnly that *now* everyone has to unwrap, and the winner is the first to present a rewrapped roll of paper!

(If you decide to play this game, do not try to follow its undoubted success with another spontaneous game. The second one will probably not work, and thus dull the impact of the first.)

'Mental' Entertainment

'Heads, bodies and legs' and quizzes really come into the category of party games. Again, such entertainment can be planned or spontaneous.

Some ideas for planned mental entertainment can include card or board games, Trivial Pursuit, or charades. If you intend to spend the whole evening on such entertainments, let your guests know beforehand so that can opt out if they wish.

As far as spontaneous mental entertainment is concerned, here are some ideas:

1 Following the lines of some successful television and radio shows, play 'Give Us a Clue' (one-person charade) or 'Just a Minute' (talk for a minute on a given subject without deviation, hesitation or repetition).
2 Word derivations. Take it in turns to think of a word and the one who gives its source most correctly gets a point (you need to have a good dictionary as reference).
3 Where is it? Think of a place and see who can guess where it is (you need a good atlas, with gazetteer).

Live Entertainment

Well, if you never want to see that friend again you can always hire an expensive 'singing telegram' to arrive in an advanced state of undress at the birthday man's private table in a famous restaurant...

Seriously, live entertainment is often the answer to the party-giver's prayer. Children's parties, for instance, are often much better with a professional conjuror (see page 62), and teenagers enjoy a disco with professional disc jockey.

If you giving an adult party and you want professional live entertainment, do *see it first*—just to check on quality and good taste!

You may, of course, have guests who have terrific talents. Ask them if they will perform—but do not badger them.

Outside Entertainment

This is a wide category that covers taking everyone to the theatre, local swimming pool or casino. If you decide on such entertainment, here are some pointers:

1 Make sure that everyone knows what is planned so they bring suitable attire (e.g. swimwear).
2 Keep a close check on time, having allowed some to spare. If you plan a theatre party with dinner first,

someone is bound to be late, or you may not be able to park. Give yourself extra time so that you don't reach your destination late, flustered and annoyed. Also, do not give people too much to drink beforehand—you don't want them to sleep their way through what might be an expensive evening!

Chapter Ten
CLOTHES

Try to provide some variety in your clothing. Everyone likes the excitement of what everyone else is going to wear.

This applies to men as well as women. Even 'black tie', called variously 'dinner jacket', 'dj' or 'tuxedo', has its variations. At such a function you will find men in black jackets, black bow-ties and no waistcoats, brocade jackets with blue bow-ties, red jackets with white cravats....

(Note to all men: 'black tie' can mean almost anything as long as it is not a conventional suit with ordinary tie!)

As host, if there might be any doubt you should give your guests a clue about dress. Tell them what you will be wearing, and they can take their lead from there.

CLOTHES

As a guest, if in doubt beforehand, ask. If you arrive at the party absolutely unsuitably dressed, there is nothing you can do about it. It is generally better to be under-rather than over-dressed, but you need more than average poise to cope with the kind of occasion where you turn up in old cord trousers and everyone else is in full evening dress.

It is more difficult, incidentally, for men. That misleading word 'informal' for instance, tells women not to wear full evening dress. But does it tell men to wear black tie (as opposed to morning dress), or sweater rather than collar and tie, or what? If in doubt, a man should ask beforehand.

The best-dressed person is likely to be one who has adaptable clothes.

I asked Roland Klein for his suggestions for the 'ideal all-purpose party wardrobe', that is to say, half a dozen garments that would see a woman of 25-40 through most types of parties:

> I think you should plan your party clothes shopping. First, go to your cupboard and see what you have there. Anything you do not wear, give away or sell. When you are left with a certain number of pieces, see what you need for a versatile party wardrobe.
>
> Ask yourself what kind of parties you may go to. Do you travel?
>
> Buy party *separates*. Whereas a dress might look right once, people will recognize it a second time. With separates you can ring the changes. I have recently designed a quartet consisting of jacket, T-shirt, skirt and trousers.
>
> Separates are more difficult as they require you to decide what to put together with what, but you will do much better in the long run. You want to be able to put clothes on and feel confident, and forget about what you are wearing.

Chapter Eleven
AFTERWARDS

Clearing Up

All good things have to come to an end and, afterwards, there is bound to be a reckoning. In the case of most parties, this takes the form of clearing up. Some people regard the washing-up after a supper party as part of the enjoyment of the whole thing. This is the time for the hosts to relax and discuss what happened during the evening. Others hate the aftermath and spend the whole evening worrying about what they will have to do afterwards.

If you hate clearing up, why not admit it and get someone else to do it? If you are organizing a community party, for instance, delegate someone else to be in entire control of the clearing up—and leave them to it. If you are entertaining in your own home and you do not have anyone in the kitchen while the party is going on (see 'staff' page 13), be strong-minded and leave everything until either your help arrives the following day, or you feel able to cope with it.

If guests offer to help, let them. Even if they put things in the wrong place, they are only doing their best. Appreciate what they are doing.
Note: do not 'clear up' too obviously while your guests are still around, unless this is one of your ploys to get rid of unwanted company (see pages 13-15).

Thank-Yous

Local areas have different customs. In the Netherlands and in the Lebanon, for instance, flowers sent the following morning are really appreciated.

Different parties have different customs too. After a bar mitzvah the young man will probably write to thank the guests for their presents, as would a bride. After most parties, however, it is generally the rule that guests thank the host.

Personally, my guidelines are these:

1 After giving a lunch at home, I do not expect a thank-you unless I happen to see my guests later, in which case a verbal 'thank-you' is much appreciated.
2 After hosting a lunch in a restaurant, I do expect a thank-you letter. The meal may have cost me a lot of money.
3 After a dinner party, or even a casual supper, I similarly expect thanks.

There are various levels of thanks: you can see my own thoughts on page 19.

Note: do not give verbal thanks for a party in front of people who were not invited.

Chapter Twelve
ALL KINDS OF PARTIES

Activities Parties

Most parties involve some kind of activity, even if it consists of merely opening your mouth at regular intervals to force in yet more food. On the whole, however, an activity party means some special activity, be it games or other entertainment.

Why not have an activity party to help with a large chore? As in the case of washing up dishes, doing someone else's is always more enjoyable than doing your own!

You can ask people to:

Help paint our new house
Dig up the tennis court
Chop firewood
Put up a fence to keep the poodle in

Here are some rules for the host of such a party:

1 It is essential that you tell guests beforehand the nature of the party. No-one will love you afterwards if you simply invite people to 'come over for Sunday' and then expect them to chop firewood. Guests need to be forewarned so that they can come prepared, and suitably dressed.
2 Provide all necessary tools and props.
3 Provide ample food and drink. Physical exercise may make your guests much hungrier and thirstier than you could have imagined.
4 Do not expect the standard of work to be as proficient as that of a professional team.

And here are some guidelines for the guests:

1 If asked to a specific activity party, and you want to decline, *do*. Tell the host that you would rather not come.
2 If you do accept, go suitably dressed and in the right frame of mind. Turn up on time: all the other guests might be waiting for you to hold the first fence post in position.

Teenage Activities Parties

Younger people really enjoy having some specific *raison d'être* for a party. Sports come into their own here, with such ideas as:

Tennis party
Swimming party
Croquet party
Orienteering party

The same rules and guidelines for host and guests apply.

Anniversary Parties

Positive points for anniversary parties include:

1 Remembering the anniversary
2 Planning the celebration suitably
3 Making sure all participants enjoy it.

When planning a celebration, ask whether or not the participants would actually enjoy a surprise party. If in doubt, do *not* surprise. If it is mid-week, do not plan a late-night party.

If it is just going to be you and your partner, go for unashamed spoiling. This is the one occasion in the year when you can go overboard on filet steak and Margaux. Disconnect the telephone, and wear your best dress.

If you are going out, try to go somewhere where you will not run into all the neighbours. This may be the one time in the year when the two of you can have an evening alone. Make it an anniversary to remember.

Wedding Anniversaries

1 year	Cotton
2 years	Paper
3 years	Leather
4 years	Fruit, flowers
5 years	Wood
6 years	Sugar
7 years	Wool, copper
8 years	Bronze, pottery
9 years	Pottery, willow
10 years	Tin
11 years	Steel
12 years	Silk, linen
13 years	Lace
14 years	Ivory
15 years	Crystal
20 years	China
25 years	Silver
30 years	Pearl
35 years	Coral
40 years	Ruby
45 years	Sapphire
50 years	Gold
55 years	Emerald
60 years	Diamond
70 years	Platinum

Some anniversaries traditionally become much more public occasions. Silver, ruby and golden weddings, for instance, are usually celebrated by all family members and close friends.

If you are planning a special party, try to make the whole thing thematic. Buy invitations with silver or golden decoration. Decorate the house, or wherever the party will be held, with suitably coloured flowers and decorations.

If you are asked to such a party, you should take along an appropriate gift. This doesn't have to be 'real' (silver or gold). Here are some ideas for presents:

Silver Wedding

Bottle of whisky/wine/champagne wrapped in silver foil

Stainless steel egg spoons

Pair of rose bushes with blue-tint or pure-white blooms (say Rosa Boule de Neige or Rosa Mme Hardy)

Packet of silver-paper doily mats

Ruby Wedding

Bottle of good red wine (unwrapped)

Jar of home-made redcurrant jelly (or a jam, with no pips/seeds)

Pair of rose bushes with deep red blooms (say Rosa Nuits de Young or Rosa Ena Harkness)

Golden Wedding

Bottle of Taittinger 'gold' champagne (laser-wrapped with Vasarely motif)

Bottle of whisky with golden ribbon bow

Pair of rose bushes (golden blooms, say Rosa Diorama, Rosa Sutter Gold or Rosa Peer Gynt)

Bottle of perfume

Big jar of Colman's English mustard

Afterwards, it is nice for the recipients to write a little thank-you note for all gifts received (or ask someone to do it for them). Similarly, all guests should write to thank whoever gave the party.

Ballooning Parties

The size of a balloon's gondola means that a ballooning party should be small in number, with back-up from ground personnel. A ballooning party is extremely expensive. As long as you accept that—you can have fun.

Balloonist Buddy Bombard discovered some years ago that ballooning in France is the way to combine interests in travel and food and wine—and people.

'From a low flight altitude, you can converse with people on the ground in little more than a speaking voice,' he says. 'Everyone is fascinated by balloons—

ours are colourfully decorated with flowers—and people always find time to stop what they are doing and greet us.'

Such ballooning parties are like very special package tours. You may balloon early each morning, wafting quietly over a different vineyard, and then come down for a champagne breakfast and a day of land-based touring.

For this special party idea, see addresses on page 94.

Bar Mitzvahs

These are Jewish ceremonies when boys enter into adult roles (the girls' ceremonies are Bat Mitzvahs). The ceremony generally takes place about the age of 13 or so, but adults, too, can celebrate after learning Hebrew.

The ceremony takes place in the synagogue. The Torah is read by the celebrant, who leads the Sabbath service for the congregation.

Afterwards there is generally a party, an Oneg Shabbat, usually for relatives and close friends and hosted by the parents. Long-term planning may be involved, and sometimes the party takes the form of a weekend reunion with multiple brunches, lunches and dinner dances. At the other end of the scale, however, the reception may consist merely of glasses of sherry and a sponge cake.

As someone who has been involved in many bar mitzvah parties told me, 'It can be a marvellous celebration because there are no bride and groom dividing the guests into two, as at a wedding. A bar mitzvah can combine the best of a wedding and a glorious birthday party.'

The Host

If you are planning a big bar mitzvah, many of the same arrangements as for wedding parties apply. (See Useful Reading.)

The Guest

You should take along a present. Money gifts in the number 18 or multiples thereof symbolize the Hebrew letter Chai (life); books, silver goblets and gifts relating to religion and learning are customary. Afterwards you may want to write and thank the host but, traditionally, the bar mitzvah boy will also write and thank you for your gift.

If asked to an orthodox ceremony, all adult guests should cover their heads.

Barbecue Parties

Here are some suggestions:

1 Let guests know beforehand that it is a barbecue. Women will probably not then turn up in high-heeled shoes that will sink into the grass.
2 When planning your barbecue party, consider contingency plans in case of rain. Let guests know beforehand what will happen if it rains ('If wet, in the local church hall', or 'If wet, we will telephone you to stop you coming and we will arrange another day').
3 Ask people who have initiative and do not need to be formally introduced. As host, you may well be too busy to make newcomers feel at ease.
4 Try to hold the barbecue not too far from your house or an appropriate source of good light, electric points (if required) and toilet facilities.
5 Make sure you are confident about your cooking. Do not try your first-ever barbecue in front of twenty guests—practise first!

Equipment

Gas barbecues are the most convenient. If you have one with a lid, you will be able to cook such magnificent dishes as whole barbecued turkey, chicken and salmon. It is probably not worth investing in a gas barbecue, however, unless you really do plan using it often.

Most people barbecue with *charcoal*. You need a

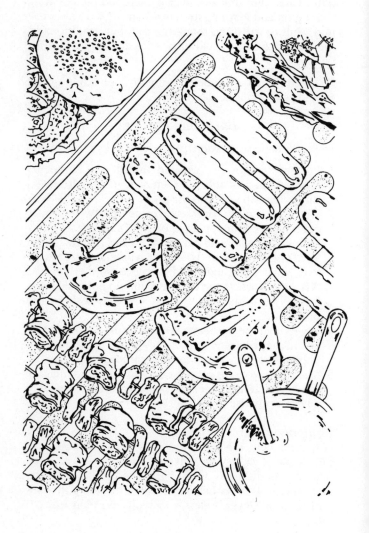

barbecue unit, say a hibachi or larger apparatus with a grill to hold the food. The quickest way of getting the charcoal to prime readiness is to lay rolls of crumpled paper over the bottom of your barbecue, put charcoal, about 3 cm deep, all over it and light the paper. Leave for 20 minutes, rake the charcoal, cover with an equal amount of new charcoal and leave for a further 30 minutes. When ready, your fire will glow red (by night) and look ash-grey (by day).

You cannot easily adjust the heat of the fire. To cook something more slowly, raise the wire grill or container holding the food.

If you use ordinary *wood*, make sure it is not a resinous pine and that it has not been treated with poisonous anti-rot and woodworm chemicals. You need plenty of wood — and time for the flames and smoke to die down.

By contrast, barbecueing with *paper* (the South African swani-brai) is an amazingly quick cook. For this you need a tall metal drum, like an old-fashioned rubbish bin with holes cut in the side as air ventilation. Crumple the sheets of a single copy of your daily newspaper into the bottom of the drum. Lay a steak with quite a lot of fat (if it is too lean, put other bits of fat with it) on a grill secure across the top of the drum. Carefully light the paper. As the flames sear upwards, the fat melts and drops down, thus fuelling the fire. Your steak will be cooked in a couple of minutes, seared on the outside, but probably still deliciously pink inside.

Food

Unless you have ample tables and chairs for everyone, try to avoid foods that need cutting up. For this reason, you may find that kebabs are easier than steaks.

Do not attempt to barbecue everything, and confine all last-minute cooking to one course. Marinate meats beforehand. Do not try to barbecue fish and meat on the same grill.

Here are some favourite barbecue foods:

ALL KINDS OF PARTIES

Starters
Babaquanoosh (aubergine dip)
Crudités and various dips
Nuts
Smoked oysters on cocktail sticks

Main courses
Kebabs
Sausages
Chops
Chicken legs
Various sauces
Baked potatoes or crisps (American chips)
Salads

Afters
Apple pie
Fruit salad
Cheese
Fresh fruit

Beforehand
Make a checklist of everything you need to think about:

Date
Time
Place
Wet-weather plans
Number of people
Guest list
Toilet facilities
Lighting (if required)
Electrical points (for coffee, etc.)
Barbecue:
   unit
   fuel
   matches
   tongs
   oven gloves
Tables
Chairs

Plates
Glasses
Cutlery
Napkins
Food
Sauces and condiments
Drinks (including mixers)
Coffee

On the Day
If the weather looks all right, go ahead! If it looks uncertain, telephone the local meteorological service and ask their advice, although ultimately only the host can make the final decision.

Set up the barbecue and all seating. Arrange the serving tables. Foods should be served near to the barbecue. Put drinks on a separate table so that people can easily help themselves (unless you wish to appoint someone bartender).

Apart from the food, make sure that everything is ready and in place in plenty of time. Give yourself a final few minutes to relax before the party starts.

At an appropriate time during the party, ask someone to help you bring out the food. Lay out all prepared foods in similar order as for buffets (See page 57).

Guests
Dress appropriately. If insects are likely to be a problem, cover up arms and legs!

Because a barbecue is generally a more informal party than one held indoors, make yourself at home and introduce yourself to others.

Beach Parties
1 The choice of beach is critical. An all-pebble beach can be cleaner, but is not so much fun. The beach should preferably be fairly private, and not too far away from the car (do not expect your guests to haul heavy ice boxes two miles over stiles and down twisting cliff paths)!

2 Good weather is essential. Do not attempt to have a beach party on a blowy night when sand is going to get into everything. If the weather looks dicey, either cancel the party or hold it indoors.

3 Choose the right type of people. Some guests simply do not enjoy the obvious work involved in a beach party and the possible inconvenience of stray sand, marauding dogs, tides coming in and too many prowlers.

4 Choose provisions carefully. Food should not be too heavy, and must not require too much preparation. If you are going to barbecue, go for 'quick cooks' (steaks) rather than 'slow cooks' (chicken halves and baked potatoes). Take plenty of drink, including lots of water.

Use plastic glasses and paper plates. Leave your best cutlery and linen at home.

Here is a checklist for the host:

Food...
Drinks
    alcoholic..
    non-alcoholic...
Corkscrew
Can opener
Paper plates
Glasses
Plastic cutlery
Bread knife (if needed)
Paper napkins
Paper towel rolls
Condiments
Barbecue equipment
Matches
Big beach umbrella
Low table (if needed)
Something to sit on (rugs?)
Something to put rubbish in afterwards

After eating, do clear up your rubbish. If there is no suitable container provided, bring all your debris home.

Note: beach parties are not the place for loud music—unless the beach is really remote.

Breakfast Parties and Brunch

A breakfast party may be a David Frost publicity-seeking early-morning business gathering. If you intend to hold such a party, make sure that all your guests are awake and alert first thing. You may do your career and friendships untold harm by inviting people for coffee and croissants at 8 a.m. when they have to drive for an hour to get there!

Anyone giving a breakfast party should also remember that many people are decidedly conservative at that meal. They might 'always eat Post Toasties', or 'have to start the day with prunes'. I remember once giving a breakfast party and being amazed that some guests wanted their jam on their ham ('We always do') while others broke their boiled eggs, as always, into the cups put ready for coffee.

Brunch, by contrast, is a more relaxed and accommodating meal. As its name implies, it is a combination of breakfast and lunch and you can serve anything from cereal and scrambled eggs through to roast beef and Yorkshire pudding—or both.

The Host

If you are planning Sunday brunch, a buffet is a good idea. People can then eat what they want (some may well have had breakfast before they came). They can also eat when they want.

Serve a choice of alcoholic and non-alcoholic drinks.

A successful Sunday brunch may well go on all day and turn into a games or activity party. Do not be surprised, however, if some people have to leave early, as they may already have afternoon plans.

Buffets

The Host

I advise anyone giving a buffet at home to follow the

logistical layouts of hotels. People need to be able to:

1 see all the foods available;
2 get to them all without a crush;
3 serve themselves without embarrassment.

Layout is important. Get pencils and paper and, literally, sketch out the progression of guests so that they move past the following in this order:

Plates
Starters
Main course
Condiments and other additives
Desserts
Cutlery/napkins (if not at table)

If you plan something extremely difficult to serve, say a whole salmon magnificently decorated, you should stand by it and do the serving, or ask someone to do it for you.

Note: do not plan a buffet if you have any guests coming who have difficulty walking or holding things steady.

Champagne Parties
(see also Drinks and Cocktail Parties)

The most exotic champagne party I have heard of for some time was that given by batik maestro Iwan Tirta in Jakarta. 'I invited seven guests to watch "Brideshead Revisited",' he said. 'We sat in my bedroom and had chocolate mousse and Dom Perignon.'

Here are some champagne recipes from Marsha Palanci of Schieffelin & Co. in New York.

For individual drinks:

Champagne Cocktail
Place a lump of sugar (half saturated in Angostura bitters) in a flute glass. Add a twist of lemon peel and fill with chilled champagne.

Champagne Julep
Place one sugar lump, one sprig of fresh mint and one

lump of ice in a large tulip glass. Pour champagne in slowly, stirring all the time, and ornament the top with fresh fruit, in season.

For larger numbers:

Champagne Cup (serves 12)
Stir into a punch bowl:

½ pineapple (in slices)
6 slices cucumber rind
1lb strawberries
4 oz Marie Brizard curaçao
1 qt soda water or seltzer
1 bottle champagne

Champagne Fruit Punch (serves 10)
Over a large piece of ice in a punch bowl, pour 1 qt of thoroughly chilled champagne. Add 1 pt soda water, ½ cup chartreuse and ½ cup brandy. Swirl the ice to chill and blend well. Add ¼ cup each of washed and halved small fresh strawberries and stemmed redcurrants.

To keep the sparkle in champagne, invest in a special stopper—available from good off-licences or liquor stores for a small sum.

For really special occasions, how about trying a champagne pyramid?

Nancy Jarratt told me about Moët & Chandon's famous *cascade*, a pyramid of hand-made crystal glasses. Many glasses are set side by side on an absolutely flat surface, with fewer and fewer glasses on top. The idea is to see how tall a pyramid you can create (Nancy says she has seen one with 1,365 glasses).

Champagne is carefully poured into the top glass. When this is filled, the champagne overflows to those beneath and so on down (One of my friends told me he did this recently in his drinks department, but, alas, a small mischief-maker pulled out one of the bottom glasses, which ruined the pyramid and resulted in a lot of broken glass!).

Ideally a *cascade* should be filled by *sabrage* (the name comes from the traditional French cavalry officer's sabre, used quickly to slice the neck cleanly off a bottle).

Children's Parties

I do not have children so, following the premise that it is always a good idea to go to someone who knows more about a subject than I do, I spoke to children's expert Diana May.

'Parties seem to have been invented for children,' she said. 'Young people are so spontaneous and fun-loving, and yet so demanding.'

Unless you are confident of ready-made entertainment —an open-air swimming pool or a first-class entertainer, for instance—the great secret of entertaining children is preparation: Spend time and thought on planning as much as possible in advance.

Your plans will depend on:

1 The age of the children invited.
2 Whether or not parents are invited.
3 Where the party is to be (in a hired hall or at home).
4 Whether or not it is a theme party.
5 Whether you plan an outing instead of a traditional party.
6 What help is available.

Age

Really young children (under four) should have *simple* parties. For them, a tea-party with just grandparents or a few chums and mums will suffice. Anything too large or ornate can be merely frightening. It is a good idea to have a few balloons and a special tea with crisps, jelly, hundreds-and-thousands on bridge rolls and the highlight of a cake with candles for everyone to help blow out. A few gentle non-competitive games such as 'Hunt the Slipper' or 'The Farmer in his Garden' can be fun.

As the children get older you are into the heavy

business of really organized parties, with games and prescribed food (see page 63). Then they grow into 'double figures' and a new sophistication that demands either outings to the latest musical or the most insistently advertised hamburger place, or wild noisy discos. Outings may be easy and actually even fun for the parents, but it can be expensive to entertain many guests. Discos have the virtue of entertaining larger numbers, but they require quite a feat of organization (see Teenage Parties).

Theme Parties

Parties can celebrate not only birthdays but also such occasions as Valentine's Day, Easter, Midsummer, Hallowe'en, Fireworks Night, Christmas and New Year. You might, alternatively, choose your own occasion (a favourite doll's birthday or a 'welcome to the new puppy' party). Such themes as a tramps' ball or a space party can also be popular (try adapting some of the ideas on page 74).

If you do decide on a special theme, follow it through from invitations to dress, décor, food, games and farewell gifts.

Summer Parties

How lucky you are if family birthdays fall in summer and you can hope for an outdoor party with paddling pool, swimming pool and/or barbecue. Invite parents to stay for a drink when they come to pick up the children.

Indoor Parties

If you feel you will be really cramped at home, why not hire a village hall? It may have its own well-equipped kitchen.

Entertainment

Ask friends for recommendations or look at advertisements, if you want a professional entertainer. Diana May suggests that you have a preliminary meeting to ensure duties are clearly spelt out. Will the entertainer be expected to help with tea and should going-home gifts be provided? Is the entertainer aware of the number and age of guests? Check, also, that the 'lady who does marvellous things with balloons' is not going to burst out of a cake clad in only two.

Some people feel that to hire professional entertainment is an expensive cop-out. The best thing, of course, is to have talent and co-operation in the family. Perhaps you have friends who will come and help as games monitors and competition judges. If necessary, bribe older children.

Planning

For a younger persons' party, start planning a guest list with your child about three weeks beforehand. Try to maintain a balance between the child's friends and those whom you specifically want to invite. Until the age of seven, the party will probably be mixed: after that it may become segregated until teens are reached. If you are holding the party at home, a dozen guests is a good maximum.

Buy invitations or, even better, help your child make them, by potato printing or using stickers on plain postcards. Invitations should state:

Name of host child
Date of party
Venue
Times of expected arrival *and* departure
Special instructions (bring swimming clothes, perhaps)
RSVP and telephone number.

Note: it is less hurtful to those not invited if invitations can be delivered to guests' homes rather than given out at school.

Start making lists. Get books of party games out of the library. Remember your own favourite games. Pencil-and-paper games only come into their own, of course, once guests can write. List the games you plan and what props are required (e.g. balloons, matchboxes, objects on a tray).

Make a list of food, drink and going-home presents. List all required 'clean-up' materials.

Food
Children have savoury tastes these days so have lots of crisps (American chips), nuts, cheese straws and dips. For more substantial food, go for sausages and hot dogs, hamburgers, fish or fish fingers and chips (French fries). Diana May thinks it is a good idea to have such foods first and then bring out any sweet items, say jellies, biscuits and a birthday cake. Sing 'Happy Birthday' as the cake is cut.

Note: children do not mind whether or not you had time to make the cake yourself. It is not a matter of how much time and money went into the cake but, rather, how it looks. A cake in the shape of a teddy bear is much more appreciated than an expensive white-iced cake with inscription.

Many children will not want to eat the cake now, so wrap up slices to be taken home.
For younger children, drinks should be simple and not strong-flavoured. Serve diluted orange squash. Some children may not like fizzy drinks.

The Day

When guests arrive, make sure the host says thank-you for any gifts (and put them away to be opened later). Plunge everyone straight into activity, say picking up dried peas with a straw or dressing dolls in crêpe paper. When everyone has arrived, play the main games for about an hour and then eat. Try to make the meal last as long as possible. Afterwards, have musical games or dancing. When parents arrive, hand out balloons and simple goody bags filled with a cheap toy, some sweets and a slice of cake.

Note: parents of guests should arrive at the stated 'end of party' time. If you arrive late it is quite likely your child will not be invited to that house again, and may be put on a wider 'black-list'.

Christenings

A christening party should not attempt to repeat wedding festivities. It is not necessary to have a party at all, really, and certainly the centre of attention (the baby) will not appreciate what is happening.

Now so many christenings take place during ordinary morning services that it may be easiest for the parents (or grandparents or other friends) simply to invite close family friends back for drinks or Sunday lunch. If there are other children in the party, make sure there are plenty of drinks and food for them.

If the top layer of the wedding cake has been kept for the christening party, take it out of the freezer in plenty of time and add plenty more alcohol as 'lubrication'. Put on new almond paste and icing.

Cocktail Parties

Who likes cocktail parties? Well, there are those freeloaders who either get invited or go anyway, and quite literally make a meal of it, scoffing all the food and drink they can.

In the main, however, the only virtue of a cocktail party is that it enables the host to 'pay off' a lot of necessary entertaining.

The Host

If you are giving a cocktail party, do not include friends when 'paying your dues' to business associates. They will not enjoy the party and they will not thank you.

Here is a guide to how much drink you should allow:

1 bottle of sherry per 4 guests
or 1 bottle of whisky per 5 guests
or 1 bottle of wine (70 cl) per 2 guests
or 1 bottle of champagne per 2 guests

Remember, too, to have more than adequate supplies of mixers for parties: people may prefer to drink the mixers on their own.

Note: many 'cocktail parties' today are misnomers, as hosts often serve wines or champagne rather than mixed drinks.

Coming of Age

This used to happen at 21 but now seems to be celebrated at 18 (and perhaps again at 21).

Coming of age should not be confused with 'coming out' or 'being presented' as a débutante, both of which imply presentation to the adult social world, without any legal connotation. Coming of age is allied to rights associated with age.

Many people celebrate a coming of age with a big family party, perhaps at a favourite restaurant. One young hairdresser told me how her father had invited everyone to a really posh dinner-dance as he said he did not know for certain if his only daughter was going to get married, and he wanted to be assured of giving her one good party.

If you are planning a coming of age party, approach it as you would a wedding. How many people do you want and what is your budget level? Do you want to go out or do the catering at home?

Make sure the guest list includes friends of the parents as well as those of the young person.

Community Parties

When organizing a village or street party it is essential to have one person nominally in charge who is prepared to make decisions. Leaving every decision, however small, in the hands of a committee can be extremely time-wasting. A committee or back-up is a good idea, however, as one person may not be able physically to cope with all that a community party involves—after all, this is a community function and not a one-person party!

Community parties can be used to celebrate special occasions (royal births, presidential elections, local commemorations) or simply as fund-raisers (for the local church tower or a new tennis court). The purpose of the party should be made clear at the outset.

Also, let everyone know who is organizing the party and for whom. Is it a street party (and if so, are people from the next street invited)? If it is a whole-town party, make sure that everyone knows that he/she is invited.

The main organizer and committee should plan delegation as early as possible. Decide on:

Date
Time
Place

and then start to delegate.

1 Put someone in charge of making sure the venue is suitable, with contingency plans in case of bad weather. If a marquee (tent) is required, this person should be responsible for seeing it is hired, put up, taken down and returned.
2 Someone else should be in charge of any required fixtures (chairs, tables, dance floor, etc.)
3 The food and drink supremo must decide what food is necessary and organize its preparation. If community participants are 'each going to bring a dish', make sure that everyone does not turn up with green noodles and no-one with anything to put on them. Similarly, a bar or other drink supply must be

considered and suitable provision made. It is better to have too much and return unused bottles than to run out. The 'food and drink' person should also liaise with the 'fixtures' person to make sure that one or other is responsible for supply of all necessary cutlery, crockery and glassware.

4 Entertainments and decoration should be considered. If a band is required, one person should be responsible. Check that any entertainment is not going to annoy nearby residents. Think about what type of decorations are most suitable and delegate their making and putting up. Think about clearing it all up afterwards.

5 Generally, it is better to have one person in overall charge of finance. There may have to be a 'float' beforehand in order to meet essential pre-party outlays (poster printing and so on). Let one person budget the whole event and cope with all money coming in and subsequent expenditure.

Dessert Parties

Jan Vachule is a keen cook who finds dessert parties an ideal form of entertaining for the working woman. 'You can experiment with lots of different things and get everything ready beforehand,' she says.

Dessert parties can be lower-cost than full dinner parties and can satisfy even the most difficult-to-please eater.

If you plan a dessert party, make sure that you offer a variety which includes:

At least one pie (unless you are having a pie party, in which case you should not serve anything else)

At least one fruit item (to satisfy those who normally never eat dessert or dieters). You can even put in a tablespoon of rum or liqueur or a splash of champagne without adding too many calories. (Drink the rest of the champagne with dessert.)

A variety of colours (unless you are having, say, an all-pink party, the perfect way to celebrate a baby girl's christening, complete with rosé champagne)

Something chocolate (as urbane as truffles or as comforting as brownies. Set an earthenware jug of cold milk near the latter and delight in a remembrance of things past!)

Something to 'take the sweetness away' (say, small lumps of cheese for those who want them, or a mixture of nuts—almonds, cashews and hazelnuts, spiced or natural)

Have plenty of plates and bowls. Your guests might not appreciate having to put apple pie in a bowl which has previously held their of helping of Danish redcurrant soup.

You may offer a *brut* champagne with desserts that are only moderately sweet and an extra dry, say Moët & Chandon White Star, with sweeter indulgences. Cognac pairs handsomely with chocolate—and so can champagne: try Michel Guerard's dark chocolate truffles with a *brut* champagne!)

Dinner Parties

The number of courses you will have at any party other than a drinks-only affair varies (from one upwards), but if any of these is available this is probably the order in which they are served:

Cheese (if eating 'American style', with cocktails)
Salad (if eating American style)
Soup (or appetizer)
Fish starter (sometimes called appetizer)
Main course (fish or meat, entrée or grill)
Salad
Cheese (if eating 'French style')
Dessert
Cheese (if eating 'English style')
Coffee (though if eating 'American style' this could even have been served throughout the entire meal)

(*Note:* more complicated menus might include sorbets variously throughout the meal—and a savoury after dessert.)

The Host

Work out your finalized menu and prepare a shopping list—long-term (dry goods) and last-minute (fresh meat and vegetables). Aim to cook ahead if you can, and freeze some things.

Make a list of things to do (flowers, clean house). Do potatoes the night before and soak in cold water with some milk added. Check what you are going to wear. Set the table in plenty of time.

On the day, remember to allow some extra time, in case an old friend calls for a long chat or you have to remake a mousse (don't worry—the failed one will do for 'leftovers' tomorrow night).

Dinner-Party Tables

A suitably dressed table needs to be the right height and size. As Howard Hirsch, who worked on interior designs for the Hyatt Carlton Tower in London and for the P&O luxury vessel, 'The Royal Princess', told me, chairs and their arms must also be exactly the right height. Lighting should be neither too bright nor too soft.

The table should be set attractively (with cloth or mats, napkins, salt, pepper and butter if required, centre-piece, china, all cutlery set exactly in military precision).

Colour is important. White cloth, white napkins and white china with no colour relief is formal and cold. Try to give some inviting warmth to the table (e.g. some bright flowers). Consider the colour of:

The cloth or mats
Napkins
Centrepiece
China

Since the food is not always on the table at the start of the meal, try not to rely on food to provide the colour.

As with clothing, do not introduce too many colours. Try to limit 'obvious colours' to a maximum of two. If you have a yellow cloth and your china is predominantly blue-patterned, do not have central flowers unless they are white, or the same shade of yellow or blue.

Try for variety. Aim to make each meal slightly different. Do not bore yourself, your household and your guests with the same setting meal after meal. You may not have different china, but you can change the colour of cloth, napkins (especially if they are paper) and centrepiece from meal to meal. Try changing the entire centrepiece so that variety is achieved through colour and shape and content: try switching from lunch's central flowers to supper's central bowl of fruit. Variety can be achieved by the smallest alteration: tying a differently coloured length of ribbon around napkins, as a makeshift napkin 'holder', can change a table setting.

Whether you use a full cloth or individual place-mats is a matter of preference. The beautifully ironed white damask cloth has an unsurpassed elegance, but it is impractical for everyday use.

If you do choose a tablecloth it is a good idea to ensure:
(a) that it completely covers the table;
(b) that table mats, if also used, are placed on top of the cloth only if they are complementary (do not put red-patterned mats on top of a checked cloth).

All linen should be spotlessly clean and in good

condition. Try not to have an odd assortment of mats. Place mats should be large enough to hold the entire setting, so that knives placed outside the mat do not 'rock' on the table underneath. Plastic and vinyl mats are most suitable for children and often for everyday use. 'Fun' place-mats can be quickly made by cutting out, with pinking shears, shapes from discarded light-weight clothing, particularly old summer dirndl skirts.

Everyone should have a napkin, for reasons of etiquette, and also because if you need to wipe your hand or your mouth you would otherwise have to employ a handkerchief or, worst of all, the tablecloth! Today, paper napkins are generally acceptable—and certainly preferable from a hygiene point of view unless you can afford to launder fabric napkins after each meal. (It must be admitted, though, that disposable paper napkins are uneconomic for a large family.) Try, if possible, to buy several-ply soft tissue napkins rather than the one-ply harder paper variety.

A centrepiece really livens up a table. Make sure it is not too tall, as people want to be able to see across the table. Some ideas for central decoration include:

1 Candles—make sure no drip gets on to the cloth or table (there are drip-catchers available, flat circular discs with central holes about 2 cm across through which the base of the candle goes: if you cannot find these in the shops, make some out of a plastic stationery folder). The classic three-branch candle-stick looks marvellous if either the central candle, or the two outer ones, are replaced by trailing flowers or ivy.

2 Flowers—if fresh, make sure they really are. Check that the vase is unchipped and clean. A plant in good condition lasts longer than cut flowers.

3 Fruit bowl—either fresh or dried fruits (gourds, rather than prunes!) look attractive.

4 Other ideas I have seen include a live goldfish in a bowl, and half a grapefruit, cut side down on a plate, with cocktail swizzle sticks stuck in to provide a colourful central 'hedgehog'.

Condiments usually placed on a table include salt and pepper, and butter or margarine. It is obviously preferable not to put their original containers on the table. If you want to limit the amount of fat taken, remember that people help themselves to more butter or margarine if a larger amount is placed in front of them, put out on small dishes.

Douglas Sutherland said that 'a gentleman is someone who uses a butter knife even when alone.' More practically, the use of a butter knife prevents the contamination that occurs if people use their own knives.

Except on really elegant occasions, it has always been acceptable to put narrow-necked bottles (tomato ketchup) and certain other decorative pots straight on the table. Unless you will have a messy spoon (e.g. honey or golden syrup), it is perhaps overdoing it to stand a pot on a plate.

Place-Settings

1 If there is more than one course, you are doing your guests a favour by putting out all cutlery before the meal starts. It is embarrassing, as a guest, to sit down to what looks like only one course and accept a large second helping—only to find that another four courses are to be brought on, each with its different utensils.

2 Check that each place-setting is conveniently placed, not too close and not too far away from its neighbour.

3 Make sure that each place-setting has:
mat (if used)
butter plate (if used), to left or upper left of where main plate will go
first-course plate (if put before meal starts)
napkin (placed on butter plate, on mat or in glass)
cutlery
glass or glasses, to upper right of where main plate will go

4 Do a final check that:

72

all cutlery is positioned precisely, with vertically
placed items exactly vertical and horizontally
placed items exactly horizontal

all china, if patterned, is placed with pattern facing
the person

all place settings are complete and the same.

As a guest, start from the outer utensils and work
inwards (or watch what your host does).

Serving and Clearing

If you, as host, stand and 'present' food, it should be
presented from behind the *left* of each guest and
cleared from the *right*. Drink should be poured from
the *right* of each guest. Port is always passed
clockwise—some people prefer not to let it touch the
cloth as it goes around.

(Incidentally, the leading hotel school, in Lausanne,
describes the ways of serving food as:

American style—'plated', with each person's food
brought from the kitchen already on his plate.

English style—the dish is presented to the host, who
then serves everyone else.

French style—the dish is presented to the host, who
serves himself, and thereafter to each guest.

Russian style—everything is brought to the table on
serving platters and served by a waiter to each guest
individually.)

When clearing plates from the table, try to avoid the
'scrape and stack' system (noisily scraping and piling
used plates one on top of another), as it will offend
many guests (particularly Americans). It is a simple
matter to stand up and carry each plate at least away
from the table (say to a sideboard) before stacking. If
there are several guests, someone will probably offer to
help you.

The Guest

If you accept an invitation to a dinner party you

definitely should go. Find out beforehand what to wear and what time to turn up (see page 17) and, afterwards, thank your host as appropriate.

Engagement Parties

These really belong to the world of weddings—see page 93.

Fancy Dress Parties

I asked actress and television star Patricia Hodge what was her favourite party. She told me:

> One of the most glorious parties of the decade was held by Nicholas Haslam in his Charles II Hunting Lodge in Hampshire. It is a National Trust property formerly lived in by John Fowler and Nicky's own genius for decoration of both house and garden provided an exquisite setting for a perfect midsummer celebration. The invitation read 'Tenue de Chasse', and guests arrived as everything from Botticelli huntresses to Inca warriors. A vast pink-and-white garlanded marquee dominated the grounds, music both ancient and modern was played, a Victorian breakfast was served all night long and fireworks were set off before dawn. Unforgettable.

The thought of fancy dress can cause some people total paroxysm. Diana May has given a lot of fancy dress parties and says that dressing up is apparently something that you either like or loathe.

Diana suggests that fancy dress parties should revolve around a theme, say a particular colour, a country, a period of history, or a certain category.

> A theme you could go for is a silver-and-gold party so that guests turn up in lamé or as knights-at-arms or spacemen. Other colour combinations are red, white and blue, black and red, and yellow and orange. You can then colour-co-ordinate invitations, décor and lighting. Alternatively, you could request national costumes of one particular country, or any country of the guest's choice. A French evening could feature guests in berets and striped jerseys having wine and cheese to the accompaniment of an accordion player.

Other ideas include a Fifties party, with women in circular skirts and men in teddy-boy drapes. A Roman orgy can prove popular, with white sheets, laurel wreaths, and quaffing from goblets while lying on one's side on sofas or the floor.

Diana also suggests asking guests to come as famous pairs (Napoleon and Josephine, Laurel and Hardy). You could also ask them to come as literary characters (Black Beauty or the Hobbit?), or musical personalities (Elvis, Madame Butterfly or Liberace).

If you are invited to a 'theme' fancy dress party, do go along with the spirit of the occasion. If you feel embarrassed about travelling on the bus in a white sheet, wear ordinary clothes, and dress when you get there.

If the invitation simply states 'fancy dress', with no theme, what should you do? If you are going as a part of a pair, do consult your other half and plan something together. Choose an outfit that you will feel comfortable wearing, and one that will not embarrass your host or any guests known to you.

Assemble everything in plenty of time. Do not leave your arrangements until half an hour before you are due to leave, as it will probably then be impossible to find a black face mask in your local shop.

Garden Parties

Garden parties are some of the most enjoyable community parties. The name evokes wistful thoughts of band music in the distance and strawberries and thick Devonshire cream with tea and cakes.

You may be lucky enough to go to a Royal Garden Party. Every year men and women from all over Britain—and further afield—are invited. You cannot ask for an invitation. If you are invited, you may be able to take a guest. You should accept as soon as possible and start planning your outfit.

If you have uniform (Red Cross, for example) you should wear that. Otherwise, a man will feel most at ease in full morning dress or national costume. Women should wear hats and cover their upper arms and, ideally, carry umbrellas (there is little rain cover convenient to Buckingham Palace Gardens). Avoid spiky high heels.

There will be several hundred people there, and traffic lines waiting to drive up to the front gates of the Palace can be extremely long. I would advise you to walk, as it saves time, and anyway it is great fun to walk across the gravelled courtyard, with all the camera-wielding tourists on the other side of the railings, wondering who you are.

It used to be etiquette, incidentally, for all women guests to wear tights or stockings and gloves, but in the heat a few years ago the Princess of Wales broke with tradition by appearing at a Royal Garden Party bare-legged. Do not follow her lead, however, unless your legs are St Tropez-brown.

Note: if you are going to a Royal Garden Party, do not forget your invitation. You will not be allowed in without it.

The Host
On a more mundane level, if you are planning to give a garden party, you may find that some of the guidelines set out under Barbecues and Community Parties are helpful.

Going-Away Holidays
My dream is to make enough money to invite ten of our best friends to join us at Mount Kenya Safari Club in Nanyuki, right at the foot of Mount Kenya....

You might decide on a less costly party. Perhaps you want to invite a couple of friends to join your holiday and celebrate your birthday. If this is the case, you as organizer (rather than 'host') should make it quite clear how much you are going to pay for, and what it will cost the others. Do not let them assume that you are going to come up with the air fares (unless you are).

You need to know someone very well to go away with them. Travelling with 'almost-friends' can be disastrous to a relationship—as we discovered many years ago when we travelled with work colleagues in Iran, and found that hitherto-agreeable people had an annoying habit of always being late for everything.

Graduation

This section applies particularly to the United States and such countries as the Philippines, where graduations are celebrated at every level of education.

My nephew Tarek graduated a couple of years ago from pre-school in Washington DC. He was then five! He had an official ceremony, wearing white mortar board and gown, and he was given a diploma scroll.

At that age a celebration party is barely appreciated. Later graduations, especially from high school at the end of twelfth grade (probably at seventeen years of age), and from college four years later, are good opportunities for parties.

Perhaps parents will offer to send the graduate on a long vacation or a big trip instead of a party. Others may decide to give a party to 'welcome the graduate home'.

Note: if you are invited to a graduation party, or if you are related to or a close friend of a graduate from high school or college, you should give a gift of about the same kind of value as you would at a coming of age.

Hallowe'en Parties

Traditionally, 31 October is when everything that is ghouly or ghostly is celebrated. This is the occasion for adults and children alike to dress up as witches, devils, bats or cats.

Decorate the house with hollowed-out pumpkins, with holes cut for eyes, nose and mouth. Put a burning nightlight inside.

Concentrate on as many browns, oranges and blacks as you can.

Caroline Conran's suggested menu for a Hallowe'en party is:

Pumpkin soup
Corn on the cob (American 'corn')
Home-cooked Boston baked beans
Devil's food cake
Pecan pie
Brownies
Popcorn
Gingerbread men
Peanut ice-cream

(All recipes are given in Terence & Caroline Conran's *The Cook Book*, Mitchell Beazley.)

House Parties
A house party does not have to include lots of guests. The minimum is technically one person staying overnight.

The Host
The best host is the one who makes his guests feel completely at home. As guest, I always thoroughly appreciate a warm welcome after a long drive. It is good if there is hot water for a bath or shower, something to eat and drink, and a chance to change and rest before 'anything happens'.

The ideal host tells his guests any 'house rules' ('Please don't leave the back gate open'; 'We usually have breakfast at nine'), and does not mind if his guests put forward specific suggestions or requirements.

Hosts should always let their guests know what is expected of them and when. It is a tremendous help to guests to know what time (approximately) meals are so that they can relax and 'do their own thing' in between.

It is also a useful social aid if the host can write down names—with correct pronunciations—of anyone else the house guest might meet during his stay.

If the host is himself invited out, he should judge whether to ask if he can take his house guest, whether to refuse the invitation or whether simply to go, alone. It all depends on how well he knows his house guest and the sender of the invitation.

The Guest

Staying overnight has tremendous responsibilities. Generally hosts are busy running their house, and cannot entertain you all day long. Be prepared to look after yourself, but if you leave the premises do let someone know where you are going and when you expect to be back.

Try to help as much as you can—but not too much. Do not fuss around the kitchen all day long. Sometimes taking home repairs into your own hands is not appreciated. Good friends of ours once had a house guest who went round and oiled all their squeaky doors—and they were furious as he had not asked their permission!

Offer to pay for telephone calls. This is especially easy in the US and other countries where bills are monthly and each call is exactly itemized. Leave a list of the numbers you have called and a cheque or money to cover the amount. In other countries (such as Britain, with frustrating three-monthly unitemized bills), you simply have to judge how much your calls might have cost. In any event, leave too much rather than too little.

If there is live-in staff, ask your host what the expected form is. Should you leave your bed unmade or not? Should you tip, and if so, how much? Never tip without asking your host's advice.

Generally today you are responsible for your own bed. Ask your host how she would like it left. Some are adamant that they do *not* want all bedding neatly piled, military style.

As a house guest wanting to slim, make sure you have your own supply of 'allowed' foods. I always travel, for instance, with a supply of bran biscuits and some fresh fruit—say a banana and a grapefruit. I can fill myself up, in my room, before joining the others at the table, when I eat very little.

Take a well-thought-out house guest present (veer towards generosity rather than meanness). Do not take food that has to be eaten immediately. Your host may have all meals planned and will not appreciate the appearance of a fresh salmon mousse.

After your visit, write a personal letter of thanks as soon as you can.

Lunch Parties

I remember walking down Fifth Avenue in New York some years ago when suddenly, in a bookshop window, I saw two people having lunch! It was a publicity venture for a new book on the subject and the poor author, apparently, was subjected to an all-day public lunch. Her guests had the good fortune to do only a one-hour stint each!

Lunch is special for many reasons:

(a) Many women find it is the only time when they can escape family responsibilities.
(b) They can more easily see their women friends (perhaps for a good talk) then.
(c) Men, similarly, may find it is the only time to see men/business associates.
(d) Lunches today are also good from a health angle, as they can be lighter than evening meals.

(e) From a budget point of view, lunches can be less expensive to give.

(f) Entertaining at lunch usually involves a certain time limit, as most guests have something to go on to afterwards.

If you are entertaining at home for lunch, here are some ideas:

1 Have a friend whom you have invited simply 'to come and keep you company'.
2 Invite several friends in and make a large pissaladiere (like pizza), or hot goulash, or something simple. Go to trouble beforehand, but not after your guests arrive.
3 A really full-scale lunch party. This can either be traditional—in which case nothing beats the traditional Sunday Lunch—or it can be offbeat, say a curry extravaganza or a cook-it-yourself Singapore Steamboat.

New Year's Eve Parties

New Year is celebrated around the world, and some festivities can go on for days. In Scotland, for instance, Hogmanay may be celebrated much more enthusiastically than Christmas, and as well as a party on 31 December it is important that as soon as midnight comes you go round to friends' houses, 'first-footing'—bearing the traditional piece of coal.

In some countries New Year's Eve celebrations have been considerably curtailed of late by strict drink-driving laws.

The Host

If you are planning a big celebration, do think about how people are going to get home. Can you ask people to stay the night? Are there good local taxi companies?

Could you employ a couple of trusty local students, paid extremely well not to drink and to drive your guests home afterwards?

As host you bear responsibility for your guests until

they get home. Whatever food and drink you plan, make sure that there is enough 'filling' food, and that the drink is 'clean'. Try not to serve both spirits and wines, and certainly do not serve an innocuous-looking but highly alcoholic punch.

Your guests might have eaten so well by the time New Year arrives that the last thing they want is a gargantuan spread revolving around—guess what—roast turkey and Christmas pudding. If you must serve turkey, try to do something imaginative with it.

The best New Year's Eve parties I have been to were given by a couple who have a large house, get in plenty of wine and have a big ongoing buffet so that guests can help themselves whenever they feel peckish. The party starts late, so that when midnight comes the guests are still in great form. By comparison, the worst I have ever gone to was a formal sit-down occasion, starting early so that there was a long, boring postprandial gap before midnight struck.

The Guests
As soon as you know your New Year's Eve plans, start thinking about babysitters. This is the worst night in the year to find someone who is not already engaged.

If you have to make your own way home after the party, decide beforehand who is going to drive. That person *should not drink at all* (if necessary, other guests could pay him, say with a bottle of consolation whisky that he can sample the following day).

This is your chance to dress up. If others are going to be wearing black tie, men should do likewise. Women can go all out with gold, glitter and jewels—and do not worry if someone else turns up in blue jeans.

Note: 31 December is also a night out for burglars. Make sure your house is well protected.

Office Parties
Office parties are usually held just before Christmas when there is too much partying going on anyway.

People are often the worse for wear even before the party starts.

At the office party, tradition used to have it that the quiet bespectacled typist wore a low-cleavage dress and lost her virtue to the personnel officer behind the filing cabinets. Nowadays, fortunately, people generally avoid such professional pitfalls.

If you are asked to an office party, remember that others will later remember how you behaved. You cannot perhaps enhance your professional reputation, but you can dramatically lower it. Do not wear anything outrageous, and do not drink too much. If you think it a good idea eat something (say a yogurt) before you go, and drink lots of water to act as a base.

If you have to organize an office party, remember to provide plenty of non-alcoholic drinks and food. Try to avoid mixed punches which contain 'unseen' alcohol.

As guest or organizer, think about transport home afterwards. Would it be a good idea to organize joint taxis so that people don't have to drive?

Older People's Parties

Hilary Wharton runs an old people's residential home and she says that one of the most popular meals of all is traditional 'fish 'n chips'. Even if you do not have a fish and chip shop or travelling van near you, cooking fish and chips today is much easier, thanks to pre-battered fish fillets and oven chips.

Another favourite main dish is scrambled eggs. For a birthday party recently, she served:

Prawn cocktail
Scrambled eggs on toast with tomato garnish
Birthday cake (very important)

Older people love going out to eat. They enjoy being invited out for tea or a simple meal—and they like being near children.

If there are party games, remember that some older

people have disabilities. Their sight, hearing and mobility might mar their enjoyment of participation.

They like a chance to dress up in their best clothes. Older women enjoy putting on their jewellery—and their 'smell'.

Picnics

All picnics should be memorable. Here are some different types of picnic.

1 A snack meal eaten in or by the car *en route* to somewhere, in preference to stopping at a motorway service station or convenient restaurant. Ideas: do not put any garlic or strong onions in the sandwiches, or everyone in the car afterwards will suffer. Provide some moist hand towelettes to prevent the car becoming greasy/dirty/oily.

2 Simple, super food, served spontaneously in a smashing environment. Ideas: on a beautiful summer evening, grab whatever is to hand (a whole smoked chicken, fresh brown bread, a bottle of wine, two glasses and some paper napkins) and go and watch the sunset.

3 A planned picnic, with carefully thought out menu. You may need wet-weather contingency plans.

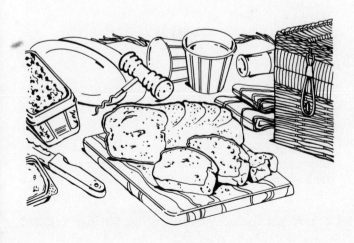

Food

I asked food writer Claudia Roden to share some ideas for picnic foods.

> My favourite picnic foods at the moment are fish and seafood salads dressed with an oil and vinegar dressing or a mixture of ginger juice and tamarind, and cold vegetables cooked in oil. Where there are a lot of us, I often do rice and cracked wheat salads. They fill people up and they are marvellous if they are mixed with chopped up raw vegetables and nuts.

> Most picnic foods make good buffet dishes—which is just as well, as with the British climate we often have to resort to eating indoors!

(Claudia Roden's book *Picnic: Complete Guide to Outdoor Food* (Penguin) is published in the USA under the title *Everything Tastes Better Outdoors.*)

Here is a checklist for most picnics:

Food containers (hamper, plastic boxes)
All main foods (make a list)
Bread, butter
Condiments, sauces, sugar, milk
All necessary drinks (with mixers)
Plates/bowls
Cups and saucers
Glasses
Necessary cutlery
Serving utensils and bread knife
Napkins
Tablecloth
Seating
Table
Can opener
Corkscrew
Moist towelettes
Rubbish container
Camping gaz or barbecue (where necessary)
Lights or torch (where necessary)

Sherry Parties

Sherry parties are usually less formal than cocktail

parties. They are a good way of returning hospitality and getting to know someone new.

Here are some guidelines for the host:

1 Do not invite more people than your house can cope with.
2 If you invite people who cannot stand for long, make sure there is plenty of seating, and somewhere for guests to put down drinks.
3 Provide *good quality* sherry.
4 And, since some people do not like sherry, have an alternative handy.

The Guest
If you have accepted the invitation, you should definitely go. Turn up more or less on time and do not expect lots of food.

You are not usually expected to take a gift and no thank-you note is required.

You can later repay the hospitality with a similar type of invitation (another drinks party) or a more lavish invitation, say to a dinner party.

Showers
Essentially an American phenomenon, these are normally women's parties, given in honour of a bride-to-be or an expectant mother—or someone moving into a new house.

They are usually held in the daytime, without complicated food. In effect elaborated girls' talk-sessions, brides' showers evolved from earlier days when a future bride might show her friends her future trousseau and the things she had made and collected for her home.

Supposing Nancy, soon to be married, has an aunt who wants to give a shower, say for ten people. Nancy will give her aunt the names and addresses of friends whom she would like invited—they do not have to be known to the host.

Showers usually have themes, say a 'kitchen shower' or an 'all-blue shower', and all guests should bring along an appropriate gift in this case something for the kitchen or something blue.

(If you are invited to a shower, you are definitely expected to take along a suitable gift, and you should write to the host afterwards.)

Sickroom Parties

If someone is ill then it may well be best not to have a party. If, however, the patient is bedbound but feeling all right, a party might be just the thing to cheer him up. (Consult your doctor if you are in doubt.)

In the case of a sickroom party, keep everything in moderation. Do not offer foods that are messy, and only serve alcohol if it is permitted to the patient.

Some invalids tire easily, so try not to let the party go on too long. 'Enough is as good as a feast' is a suitable maxim for the sickroom party.

Sunday Lunch Parties

The appeal of Sunday brunches is covered on page 55. By contrast, others like to entertain with a traditional cooked Sunday lunch, possibly the one time in the week when a whole family sits down together to a hot meal.

It is not a good idea to schedule a pre-lunch drinks party, with only a few of the guests invited to stay on for lunch itself. There are always one or two drinks-only guests who do not 'get the message', and if you are planning a rare beef roast you might eventually find yourself sitting down to charcoal at five o'clock.

The good host invites guests to a Sunday lunch party in plenty of time to have a drink before the meal.

The Food

This is the occasion for plain traditional food, say roast lamb with gravy (brown sauce) and mint sauce or redcurrant jelly, rather than the garlic-studded pink lamb with gooseberry purée which might be more appropriate for a dinner party.

My own favourite Sunday lunches are those where real 'nursery food' is served, with the roast meat and 'two veg.' followed by apple crumble with really yellow custard!

The Guest
It is a real honour to be invited to share a family's Sunday lunch. Make sure you turn up on time. If there are children present, try to bring them into the conversation.

Tea Parties
Did you know, tea is in? In some houses tea as a meal has never been out, but, for most, a mere cup of tea sometime during the afternoon is probably all that has weathered the last few years.

Now tea and tea dances are returning in high fashion, in hotels and restaurants in Budapest, Hamburg, London and New York. Chefs vie with each other to offer silver samovars with choice of blend served by long-skirted hostesses. Guests may be offered 'traditional home-made scones with strawberry jam and preserves, shortbread and cherry cake'.

The trouble is that most people want simply a cup of tea. So, for hosts holding tea-parties in their own homes, here are some guidelines:

1 Provide plenty of tea. Even guests who normally never touch the stuff can drink several cups at a party. Ideally, give a choice of teas, and offer both thin lemon slices and milk.
2 Do not provide enormous amounts of food unless you are entertaining your weightlifting friends, and do not be upset if some guests eat nothing at all.

The Guest
Enjoy yourself, but do not eat unless you really want to. Your host will quite understand.

Teenage Parties

If you are shuddering at the thought of hosting a teenage party, be consoled by the fact that every adult has qualms before and during such an event. Miraculously, however, most teenage parties go off without a hitch.

Subtle organization is the key to the whole thing. Take some tips from 'professional organizers', people like school housemasters who have parties for their students. They plan beforehand, with some of the students. As much furniture as possible is removed before the party starts. People are delegated to clear up afterwards.

It is much easier to give a joint party so that several teenagers and their parents share responsibility (although only one household, of course, will bear the brunt of any damage).

Talk to the person for whom the party is being given and find out what he or she wants. Do you—and they—want the same kind of party?

Decide together when and where the party will be, and who will be invited (do you know the names, including family surnames, of all those coming?). Bear in mind that few will answer the invitation and your original guest list will bear no relation to who actually comes. Parties in cities and towns are more likely to attract gatecrashers than those in rural areas. Agree what time the party will end, and stick to it.

These are 'dress-down' parties. Some guests may well look like vagrants.

Food is unimportant. There is no point in providing elaborate buffets: you will do better to stick to masses of nuts and crisps or, at the most, fish and chips. Drink, on the other hand, *is* important. Regardless of what you serve, guests are likely to bring their own supplies (half a bottle of spirits is not out of teenagers' financial reach) and they may well mix their drinks indiscriminately. Provide plastic glasses, as anything broken is unlikely to be removed until morning and you do not want to be responsible for cut feet.

Remember that others' smoking standards may be not as stringent as your own. Even if you provide ashtrays some guests may well prefer to stub out their cigarettes on your best sofa (memo: remove all valuable or vulnerable furniture!).

Do not try and organize entertainment other than self-help or commercial discos. In many cases a dance floor is left deserted while guests remove to other rooms, to drink or socialize in pairs in dark corners. If the party looks like being noisy, warn neighbours beforehand, and tell them what time the party will end.

Experienced partygivers agree on the usefulness of appointing a couple of older guests as 'wardens'. If you are not in the house, make sure they have your telephone number.

It is quite possible that many guests will want to stay overnight. Ask them to bring their sleeping bags—and mobilize their help the following morning in clearing up. If they are not staying overnight, make sure that transport is available, in case they are not in a fit state to drive.

* * *

Why give such a party? Those who know say that it is sometimes essential for a teenager to take his turn as host, and invariably it is parents who have to suffer afterwards.

There are, fortunately, alternatives to the nightmare 'teenage party' described above:

Theatre party, or visit to see a good show
Barbecue
Activities party
Small formal dinner party (when the same teenagers who 'dress down and act badly' at a general party may enjoy dressing formally and relish the whole concept of good food, drink and conversation)

Some teenagers, too, will come into contact with *coming-out parties*, today more often arranged for the delight of mothers than that of daughters (as most young women today would die rather than be called débutantes). Some parents decide to have a cocktail party for their children and, perhaps, take a small number of friends to the Rose Ball.

(For help, you can contact Mr Peter Townend—address on page 95).

Theatre Parties

Going to a show is a marvellous form of activity party—but an evening show raises the big problem of when to eat.

The Host

Frankly, at a theatre party, food should take second place. Do not plan a three-course meal before going to the show. Ask your guests to have a snack beforehand and meet you at the theatre. Let them know that you have booked a table at a seafood restaurant afterwards.

The Guests

Turn up exactly on time at the host's house or the theatre, as appropriate. Do not take along chocolates with noisy wrappings: you will make yourself very unpopular with the people around you.

If there seems to be an opportunity, offer to buy programmes, and drinks during the interval.

A theatre visit is a high-cost event, especially if an expensive meal is included. Write and thank your host afterwards.

Wakes

In many areas, it is still not uncommon for close women relatives of the deceased not to go to the funeral but to stay home and prepare the meal. Elaborate presentations of home-cooked ham and green peas and lots of desserts might be served.

The Host

Someone should offer to entertain mourners, who might have travelled quite a distance. One of the most moving wakes I have been to was a strawberry tea. It poured with rain and we were not able to go into the magnificent garden but there was plenty of room inside the house. It was a suitably simple meal, but stylish.

The Guests

Much of the initial mourning will be over, and the post-funeral party is not the time for obvious lament. There is no need to avoid reference to the deceased but, on the other hand, try to behave as normally as possible.

The party has probably been arranged at extremely short notice and your help might be appreciated, in pouring tea or drinks and passing round food.

Do not outstay your welcome. Family members may need to discuss important business after other guests have left.

Weddings

The world of weddings warrants a book all to itself. May I therefore recommend my own book, *Getting Married*, also published by Batsford?

USEFUL READING

Conran, Terence and Caroline, *The Cook Book*, Mitchell Beazley 1980

Gostelow, Mary, *Getting Married*, Batsford 1986

Leith, Prue, *Dinner Parties*, Papermac 1986
   Entertaining with Style, Macdonald 1986

McDouall, Robin and Bush, Sheila, *Recipes from a Château in Champagne*, Gollancz 1983

Roden, Claudia, *Picnic: Complete Guide to Outdoor Food*, Penguin 1982

Spencer, Ivor, *Speeches and Toasts*, Ward Lock 1980

Wade, John, *It's Your Turn to Speak*, Batsford 1985

USEFUL ADDRESSES

Ballooning
Bombard Society, 6727 Curran Street, McLean Va. 22101 USA. Tel. *(703) 448 9407*

Château de Laborde, Meursanges, 21200 Beaune, France. Tel. *(80) 22-51-61*

Champagne Voyages de Reims, Air Show Ltd, 4 rue du Ruisselet, 51100 Reims, France. Tel. *(26) 82-59-60*

Champagne
Champagne Bureau, 14 Pall Mall, London SW1Y 5LV. Tel. *(01) 839 1461*

Champagne Bureau, Berger & Associates, 133 Richmond Street West (Suite 203), Toronto M5H 2L5, Canada. Tel. *(416) 862 0830*

Champagne News & Information Bureau, 222 E 42 Street, NYC NY 10017, USA. Tel. *(212) 907 9382*

CIVC, 5 rue Henri-Martin, 51200 Epernay, France. Tel. *(26) 54-47-20*

Coming-Out Parties

Peter Townend, 36 Chelsea Towers,
Chelsea Manor Street, London SW3 5PN.
Tel. *(01) 352 2952*

Staff

Ivor Spencer School for British Butlers &
Administrators, 12 Little Bournes, Alleyn Park,
London SE21 8SE. Tel. *(01) 670 5585*

Wines

Canadian Wine Institute, 1 rue Yonge Street (Suite
2104), Toronto M5E 1E5, Canada. Tel. *(416) 363 5769*

Cape Estates Wine Producers Association, PO Box 10,
Koelenhof 7605, South Africa. Tel. *(2232) 393*

Comité National des Vins de France,
43 rue de Naples, 75008 Paris, France.

Direct Sunday Times Wine Club, New Aquitaine House,
Paddock Road, Reading RG4 0BY. Tel. *(0734) 481713*

Malmaison Wine Club, 28 Midland Road,
London NW1 2AD. Tel. *(01) 388 5087*

Society of Wine Educators, 1048 Oak Hills Way,
Salt Lake City, Ut. 84108, USA. Tel. *(801) 582 8105*

Wine Appreciation Guide, 155 Connecticut Street,
San Francisco, Ca. 94107, USA. Tel. *(415) 864 1202*

Wine Institute, 165 Post Street, San Francisco,
Ca. 94108, USA. Tel. *(415) 986 0878*

Wine Society, PO Box 9, Gunnels Wood Road,
Stevenage, Herts SG1 3BR.

For further information on many things
mentioned in this book, and for details of Mary
Gostelow Enterprises and The Complete Woman,
please send two first class stamps to:

Mary Gostelow (PP), PO Box 135, Ringwood,
Hants BH24 1JB

INDEX